Why Do Whales And Children Sing?

**A GUIDE TO
LISTENING IN NATURE**

David Dunn

EARTHEAR

E A R T H E A R

Your ears will never be the same.

45 Cougar Canyon ▪ Santa Fe, NM 87505
toll free 888-564-3399 ▪ phone/fax:505-466-1879
www.EarthEar.com ▪ info@EarthEar.com

Design by Michael Motley, Santa Fe, NM

Illustrations within the text are adapted
from sonograms by David Dunn.

Cover calligraphy by Kazuaki Tanahashi.
The character is *voice* or *sound*.

The ancient Taoist symbol on the facing page is a
Talisman to Stop Wind (a spell dear to the hearts
of the world's intrepid field recordists...)

This book is manufactured in the United States of America
by Braun-Brumfiled. Inc. CD manufactured by ESP

Library of Congress Catalog Card Number: 99-61987

Dunn, David
Why Do Whales and Children Sing?
ISBN 0-95401-03-5
1. Nature 2. sound 3. Culture 4. Music
I. Title
1 2 3 4 5 6 7 8 9 10

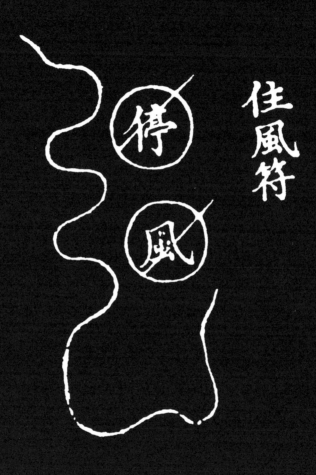

住風符

6

The following individuals have contributed to this project with advice that has been invaluable. I wish to thank them for their suggestions and friendship: Janet Bailey, Brad Brookes, Leslie Knowlton, and Robert Shaw. I also express deep gratitude for the use of their incredible sounds to Les Gilbert and Jack Loeffler. Special thanks go to Jim Cummings, my publisher and editor, who made this possible in so many ways. Most of all I wish to acknowledge the patience and incredible insight of my wife, Naomi and our daughter Katrina. This project was partially funded through a Dean's Faculty Research Grant from the College of Santa Fe.

t is indeed a treat to listen, read, and respond to this invaluable work. I've always found in David Dunn's writing a deep probing which prods me to rethink my own work with sound, but it's also been intricate writing. This book has all his depth within a transparent style – and what recordings! Gorgeous. It is a lovely contribution toward the rather large goal of reawakening our culture's dormant auditory engagement with the world.

Why do Whales and Children Sing? is a subtle, multi-layered work which seamlessly incorporates several functions in a most compelling way, becoming a powerful tool of advocacy for responsible ecological awareness and action. In the process of reawakening our ears, David guides us

7

towards the essential recognition of how deeply we are integrated into the world's community of being and how inescapably responsible we are towards it.

I have been listening to and thinking about soundscapes for many years, and yet this book is full of revelations for me. Each recorded segment is full of vitality, full of "presence". But it is his commentary which transforms it from a purely aural pleasure into something multi-dimensional. Starting with information about how we hear, he moves on to consider how other creatures create, employ, and even more interestingly, hear and respond to sounds. The particular characteristic soundmix of a location, the variables of time of day and climate affecting it and speculations about such a mix as an emergent communal mind are particularly stimulating. So he makes me think freshly about such intersections, pulls me beyond how I hear, encouraging me to reintegrate myself into this "complex chain of connection," an invaluable gift.

I became intrigued with the various ways in which Dunn

structured the book/CD's span, very much like a musical composition. The first thing to strike me was the way sonic connections are made from one cut to the next: water and thunder threaded through the first three cuts, for example. Then, like a sonic microscope, underwater communications emerge, pulling my ears into close focus. As they sharpen, he enlarges the scale, incorporating location and climate, until, when he includes human activities, I can perceive them as a part of the mix, no longer foregrounded. Another structural thread seems to be the evolutionary passage, from ocean to amphibian life, to insect forms and mammalian forms. These connective links are compelling, not least because they are not presented as staight line evolutions, but move back and forth in a supple way, not immediately obvious.

There is a welcome intellectual clarity, even rigor here, and a generosity of heart towards the listener/reader which welcome one into listening, into reflecting. Connection becomes possible.

Annea Lockwood

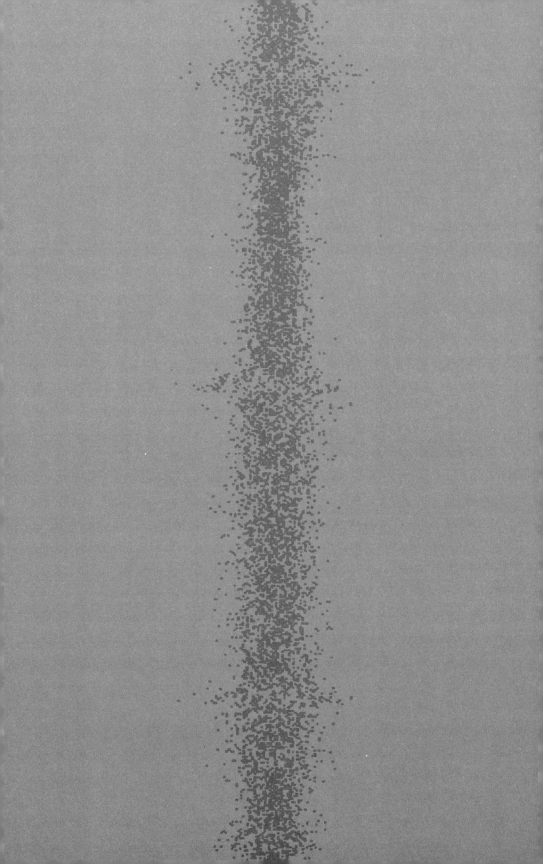

T

here are many parallels in the collecting of sounds to

other ways of documenting and "binding time" in order to

study, intensify experience, or cherish the past. The similarity

of recorded sound to photography has been articulated,

but "phonography" has yet to be taken seriously as a dis-

cipline beyond its commercial or scientific applications. Its

status as an artistic genre is still quite tentative despite the

efforts of an ever-widening cadre of enthusiasts. The rea-

sons are probably many but I want to focus on the one

that primarily informed the preparation of this book: we

do not take our perception of the world through sound

very seriously. I mean this quite literally. Most of us are

visually-oriented; we are encouraged to be so by our culture and especially the language we use to construct that culture. Visual acuity may even be a dominant trait of our species. Other than the frustration it provides for people like me who are aurally-oriented, this may not be a problem. But it does shape our day to day understanding and behavior in profound ways.

To "illustrate" the dominance that vision has in our thought processes, let's do an experiment. Listen to the sounds of your immediate environment or to a small bit of music. Now try to describe some aspects of a particular sound or a musical phrase, some qualities that it exhibits. Most people will resort to visually-based concepts like shapes in space or properties of size and direction. They will invariably describe pitch in terms of up or down when in fact sounds are determined by wavelengths that have nothing to do with how high or low they are. Try to reverse this process by using sound-based metaphors to describe something you see and most people can't. When we do, it is surprisingly satisfying: such as describing someone's clothing as loud or noisy. We have organized our culture around the dominance of the eye.

Visually-based metaphors are probably the worst for describing the density of interconnections from which the world is made. When we mostly speak of the world in topological terms that impose a fixed time/space relationship on the rich dance of living things, we constrain our understanding of the true interdependence of life. This not only has serious implications for how we relate to our environment, but also for how we come to an understanding of what we know. In Buddhism the concept of *Sunya* (a Sanskrit word translated as "emptiness") describes the complex chain of connection that forms the world. Each "thing" is so densely connected to everything else that it resides nowhere. We cannot isolate anything from all the states of matter or energy that came before or that follow. It is this understanding that Gregory Bateson referred to as the sacred: "the integrated fabric of mind that envelops us." Sound as the language of vibration is perhaps the best means we have for perceiving this fabric of mind that resides everywhere.

This concern for the sacred quality of the perception of

sound will be discussed in this book through two broad categories of phenomena: the first is the nature of communication through sound as it occurs in nature, between living things in general. The second area of emphasis will be on music as communication between humans and between humans and their environment. Music has such an important role here because of its special status, alongside spoken language, as one of the most prolific ways in which humans organize reality through sound-making. Every culture has some form of music. In later sections of the book I will present some of my ideas about why I think this has been the case and why it is of even greater historical consequence now.

Most of us constantly listen to recorded sounds in the form of music or media information. Seldom is this done with direct concentration. Usually it is to distract us from something else: entertainment as the food of depression. Most forms of music now share this trait. The merchandising of music has become what Jacques Attali has called a "disguise for the monologue of power... never before have musicians tried so hard to communicate with their audience, and never before has that communication been so deceiving. Music now seems hardly more than a somewhat clumsy excuse for the self-glorification of musicians and the growth of a new industrial sector." At a time of ecological crisis we need to embrace every tool we have that can remind us of the sacred. Not only can aural and musical metaphors provide us with a means to describe the world in ways that remind us of our physical connection to the environment, but the physical act of using our aural sense, in contrast to entertainment, can become a means for integrative meditation.

This book can be used for many purposes, including entertainment. It is my hope that it can be useful as a tool for strengthening listening skills that lead to personal ways of thinking about the world differently. Ways that place the perception of sound at the center of how we relate to the world, at least part of the time. That's also why this book has minimal illustations. It's not about packaging a bunch of interesting sounds along with visual distractions. It's about coming to a better understanding of how we listen to things.

My initial idea was to select sounds that illustrated levels of scale in nature, organized according to how big or small their sources were. I soon realized that this was not only a contradiction of the premise of this book, but was also downright impossible. Size is a visual mapping, not an aural one. I could, however, think about sound in terms of proximity to the listener. Most of the time I will be talking about sound as inseparable from a listener, focusing upon the whole pattern of relationship that the sound itself articulates. Along the way I will try to contextualize the sounds with personal anecdotes, listening guidance, and natural history details.

In no way should this book be thought of as a scientific document. I am an artist and my personal interest remains throughout to focus on the aesthetic experience of sound in natural environments. The scientific references are only intended as an additional tool for constructing subjective metaphors based in my direct experience. Given this attitude, errors are probably inevitable. While I have made sincere efforts to be scientifically accurate, readers whose primary interest is to judge such accuracy will find much to condemn. I can only say that if science was my primary motive I would have chosen a different path long ago.

The quality of listening to the natural world is different than looking at it. This is not an argument for using your ears more than your eyes or a claim that one mode of sensing is superior to another. That would simply be absurd. Rather, it is an attempt to encourage making listening a more conscious experience. When we look at the world, our sense of vision emphasizes the distinct boundaries between phenomena. We concentrate on the edges of things or on the details of color as they help to define separate contours in space. The sounds that things make are not so distinct and, in fact, the experience of listening is often one of perceiving the inseparability of phenomena. Think about the sound of ocean surf or the sound of wind in trees. While we often see something as distinct in its environment, we hear how it relates to other things. Take for instance the image of an airplane in flight. What looks like a distant pinpoint object in the sky is heard as a web of sound that spreads out through the terrain beneath it, reverberating from the contour of the land into and around our bodies.

I do not mean to imply that our hearing is somehow less discriminating than our vision. Actually, the number of nerve fibers that connect our ears to the brain is greater than the number that connects to the eyes. We can easily experience what this means: our ears are better at discriminating certain kinds of very complex phenomena and we can often hear relationships between things that our eyes require external instrumentation to accomplish. Mathematics in western culture was born from the sense of sound, not vision. Pythagoras heard the ratios of the monochord vibrating; from that perception, came arithmetic. Since then philosophers from Plato to Adorno have discussed the sacred properties and special responsibilities of sound and music to society.

Another example of how the sounds we hear articulate profound physical patterns of connection between things is the research done on the effect of sound and music on plant growth. As far back as the 1950s, botanists observed such dramatic increases in the weight and yield of agri-cultural plants exposed to audio stimulation that the National Research Council of Canada funded research into what effect sound could have on wheat seed. They found that seedlings exposed to specific frequencies of sound exceeded the weight of control specimens by 250 percent, and produced more shoots. One scientific hypothesis for the result is that the plants are in some way feeding off the sound or reinforcing the absorption of light through a resonance effect comparable to photo-synthesis. My own experiments with sound and plant growth involved the playing of heterodyning sine waves, dropped to four octaves below their original frequency and time domain, to a group of young plants. After a few hours the plants would invariably lean toward the loud-speakers in direct opposition to the windows and sunlight to which they were normally attracted.

In my work as a professional composer and sound design-er, I have gathered a large and curious collection of recorded sounds. These sounds include a vast array of music, effects for film and video soundtracks, audio samples for electronic and computer-based musical instruments, and most of all a unique assortment of nature sounds gathered over the past twenty or so years. Many of these sounds were recorded for specific projects such as exhibition enhancement in zoos and aquariums. Others were recorded for television documentary soundtracks or radio shows. Some were things I just happened upon while doing commercial recording projects. Many others are documents of my experiments as a composer exploring the interactive potential of sound in wilderness environments or are the result of scientific research. Many of the sounds were recorded by other people.

I usually thought about all these recordings as merely the consequence of what I do to make a living. But one day, while I was desperately looking for an apparently lost tape, it occurred to me that much of what was on my shelves and in boxes was not of practical value. These were recordings that I had collected out of a fascination for the sounds themselves. The recordings had taken on the character of wonderful curiosities, like the specimens in apothecary jars that once formed the basis of antique natural history studies. These specimens were the starting point for this book: meditations on a few of these sonic "objects" as documents of unique events and meaning in nature.

ABOUT THE SOUNDS:

Since the emphasis of this book is on listening to the sounds of the natural world, it might be a little confusing to realize that the recorded sound examples are illusions. Recorded sounds have the same relationship to their source sounds as photography or video does to reality. They are reproductions of the infinitely complex world collapsed into an illusion of space and time. While we are all very familiar with the framing of visual information that we see on a printed page or video monitor, it's easy to forget that the stereo image of a sound recording is a similar contrivance. The sound image formed by two loudspeakers is a fake reality just like television or movies. It just happens to be a convenient way to convey my ideas with a little more vitality than verbal description alone. Keep in mind that listening in nature is very different than what the simplistic conventions of media reproduction will allow. When listening to these sounds, remember that you are listening to a technological translation of the real world.

It might be helpful if I discuss some of the aspects of how these recordings were made. This is not a rigorous description of the art of sound recording, just a couple of vague principles that might help orient you.

When recording sounds in nature, one of the most important things to be aware of is how your presence affects what you are listening to. Proximity is a critical determinant of what you can record. Different kinds of microphones can play a role in this, in the same way that the choice of lens in photography shapes the final image. Some microphones have a greater "reach", allowing you to be selective about what you record while staying at a greater distance from the sound source. The more the microphone's reach, however, the less neutral or accurate is the recording of the sound. Microphone design and basic physics determine that the more directional a microphone is, and therefore more able to pickup sounds from a distant source, the less it is capable of responding to the full range of sound in the environment.

The placement of the microphones is the most important factor in how the final recording will be "framed." What the microphones are pointing at determines the illusion of space in the recording's stereo field. What you hear in these recordings is not only information about what was happening in the environment, you also hear how the microphones were placed in relationship to those events. In a few cases, specifically the underwater recordings, the technological medium allows you to experience sounds that your ears cannot actually hear.

Since all of these recorded sound events unfold in time within a physical location, they articulate aspects of a space/time continuum. You might even say that you can locate them on a continuum of emphasis between pure space and pure time. In some cases you are more aware of the space that an event occurs within. In others you are more aware of how the sounds announce the passage of time. For instance, #21 is somewhere in the middle. The Loon's call requires a definite time frame for us to be aware of its shape, but the long echo conveys a sense of the size of physical space within which the call is made. These relationships not only result from the balance of a sound to its surroundings, but also to the frame of reference established by the microphone placement.

LISTENING OPTIONS:

The optimal conditions for experiencing this book are probably as follows: Sit alone at a comfortable distance from your two loudspeakers, facing them in the center of the stereo field. The playback volume should be adjusted to the first example. Set the volume so that the stream is somewhat soft to your range of hearing while the thunderclap does not distort (i.e., sounds like nearby thunder). The sounds that follow will vary greatly but should be at correct levels in relationship to each other. Read the text and listen to the sound examples by selecting the proper index number on your CD player when you see the calligraphic symbol. Hit stop or pause when the selection ends. As in so many other aspects of our modern lives, a remote control helps.

There are many other ways for the reader/listener to use this book. While the sequence of numbered sections implies a linear reading from cover to cover, you can also read any section you want, listening to its corresponding sound sample individually. If you are using this book with other people, you can take turns reading the text aloud, alternating with the recorded examples. That way the whole experience can be a predominantly aural one. You can also listen to the sounds through headphones and silently read the text to yourself. With a portable CD player you can take it with you to the beach or on the subway. If you just want to hear the sounds, that's also fine. They are indexed on the disk itself. Teachers can use the book in a classroom. It can be the basis of a special gathering or you can read (listen to) a section or two a day. Don't be afraid to engage the material in whatever order seems fit, to repeat sections, or to take breaks along the way. It will all be there when you come back to it.

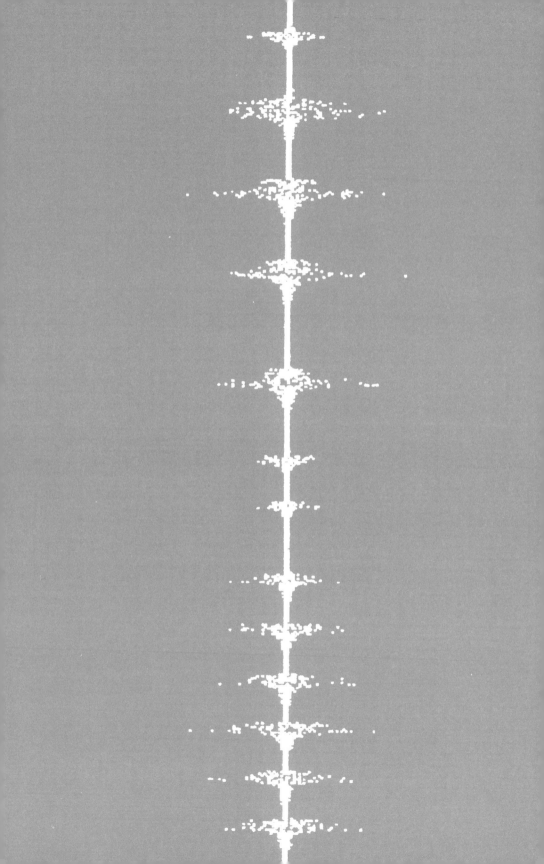

 = Listen Now!

CHAMA, NEW MEXICO:

MOUNTAIN STREAM AND APPROACHING THUNDER

We start with this recording because it seems to represent something of a cliche. It is what many people think of when they think of the recorded sounds of nature. It is even the popular plot for some Classical symphonic tone poems, including Beethoven's Sixth Symphony (The Pastoral). I include it here not only for practical reasons (it is useful to the listener for adjusting their amplifier level) but also because it is a gentle way into the generally unfamiliar sounds that follow.

What do these sounds tell us? Mostly they seem grossly familiar and cliched because of their use in movies, cartoons, new-age music, therapeutic sessions, and other contexts where they have been used to invoke "states of relaxation." They are the quintessential "sounds of nature" as if the immensity of the Earth and its inhabitants could be reduced to such an abstraction or singular state of mind. Part of what serious listening demands is the willingness to unload such projections from the saturation of popular media and commercial hype. I do not mean to imply that our projections aren't valid or that there aren't some profound reasons for associating these sounds with specific psychological or emotional states. I'm just arguing for the necessity to hear beneath the surface of our most familiar projections to what might be a more intrinsic understanding.

Dr. Alfred Tomatis has explored and simulated many sounds that the fetus hears in the prenatal sound world. He contends that the embryo begins to develop ears (meaning the complete hearing apparatus) within a few days of impregnation and completes their growth by the 135th day. In the dark ambience of the womb, floating in amniotic fluid, the fetus hears the sounds of the mother's physiology, her speech and other sounds of the outer world filtered through her body. Many of these sounds have an almost archetypal quality to them that is reminiscent of the sounds of the natural environment or music:

The mother's breathing cycle is like ocean surf and her heart beat like distant drums. Her speech sounds like the scratchy texture of an insect chorus and her digestion like the boiling surface of a small stream. These are the basic rhythms that set the pattern for our being in the world. No wonder that many sounds of the forest trigger such rich associations.

While I am not qualified to judge the scientific merit of this work, I find it invaluable as metaphor and a vigorous stimulus to my imagination. What biology has revealed, with the idea that ontogeny recapitulates phylogeny, is that fetal development in the womb exhibits structural similarities to how we understand the broader evolution of life. The fetus must, in some sense, relive prehuman evolution and it must do so by feeling and hearing it. Just as we grow through former stages of life, we may experience more primitive forms of hearing. What we "know" before we are born might be what we have heard as the retraced morphology of other forms of life on this planet. It's a wild and wonderful speculation but one that I find irresistible. Some of our most primal knowledge might be that we know how to hear like crickets, frogs, birds and coyotes.

VENICE BEACH, CALIFORNIA: THUNDERSTORM

Compare the sound of this thunder with that of the previous example. The urgency and violence of a storm come to the foreground when present in an urban context. There are no pretty sounds to soften the reality. But just what is that reality? Like all of our senses, what we hear is a combination of something out in the world happening around us, like a thunderstorm, and the organization of our physiology. We are each constructed as a miraculous community of systems that function together to form the coherent totality of a living thing capable of sensing the external world. Since that coherence is finite, there are real limits on what we can sense. All of the phenomena that we hear is only a fraction of the vibrating going on in our universe.

What we hear is the result of a dance between the world and how we are made. In a sense, we organize our reality out of this dance. Since this is true for all living things, and since each thing is made differently, each form of life hears differently. Our species, like most others, may have evolved its ability to detect vibrations within a range of 20 to 20,000 cycles per second, because that was the range of sound made by those things that either we ate or ate us. So just how do we hear the thunderstorm? Fluctuations in air molecules convey to our ears something vibrating. Our outer ear collects this noise and funnels it into the middle ear through the ear drum, a membrane that vibrates in response to the fluctuation of air. The middle ear, with a combination of bone, tissue and air, amplifies the ear drum's vibrations and passes them into the inner ear. Here a special organ called the cochlea, shaped like a spiral seashell and filled with fluid, transduces vibration into electrical impulses. The most mysterious part of this process is the part of the cochlea called the organ of Corti, a microscopic vibratory mechanism that consists of over 23,000 hair cells linked to an equal number of fibers in the auditory nerve. Exactly how these hairs convert mechanical motion into electrical current is still a controversial research topic. Once these nerve signals reach the brain, we hear the thunder.

LES MOULINS, SWISS ALPS:

COWS AND THUNDERSTORM

While hiking down from the top of an alpine mountain, my comrades and I were met on a high mountain pass by a group of cows. The wonderful contradiction in the soundscape forced us to stop while I recorded. Compared to the powerful immensity of the natural forces contained in the thunderstorm and how it resonated through the mountains, the delicacy of the cow bells seemed reassuring. Even though the bell sounds were being made by such large animals, they seemed comforting against the inhuman scale of the mountains and impending storm. The bells served to remind us of our human size and concerns, including domestic animals seeking shelter from the same intimidating forces of nature.

Sound obviously doesn't just occur in air. It also moves as vibrations through walls and rock, or through the gaseous atmospheres of distant planets. An even better medium for the propagation of sound is water, and almost all the creatures who live in water are made to hear in it.

The earliest form of ear was probably evolved in the sea and was actually a type of balance indicator rather than a hearing mechanism. This evolved over aeons into the mechanism of hearing in fish, a more generalized organ than our ears. They have no real outer ear or eardrum at all, just tiny bones connected to nerves. With a gas bladder that acts both as a float for buoyancy and as a primitive form of eardrum, they have connected balance sensing to hearing. This vibration sensor sends sound through bone and tissue to the inner ear full of liquid and nerve centers. Most fish also have what's called a lateral line on their sides that is sensitive to low frequency sounds and fluctuations in water pressure.

33

When you realize that the human ear is also an essential means for maintaining our body's balance in the world, the connection to ancient sea creatures seems resonant indeed.

Unfortunately our hearing is pretty lousy underwater, but swimmers and divers have been known to hear the loud and widespread clicking of crustaceans such as snapping shrimp. This recording is a good representation of what the ocean sounds like in many places. Rather than the silent deep, it is sometimes a cacophony so great as to interfere with Navy sonar. Some fish sounds are so loud that a fisherman can hear them above water and others, like trout, make a sound as they leap out of water.

The sounds of the underwater world are still mostly a mystery that can lead to real surprises. I once was recording the sounds of a lake in North Carolina while lounging in a canoe. My hydrophones were dangling over the side and I was beginning to fall asleep listening to the subtle underwater world. Suddenly I heard a sound of almost prehistoric dimensions, loud, low and frightening, and nearly tipped over the canoe. I later found out that catfish weighing over 100 pounds had been caught from that lake.

MAUI, HAWAII: HUMPBACK WHALES

The extraordinary intelligence of cetaceans (whales and dolphins) is legendary. Dolphins have successfully learned a whole range of ways to communicate with humans, including the imitation of human speech. These animals might rightfully claim to be the most sophisticated sound-makers on the planet since they can simultaneously carry on complex communications with each other while using sound to orient themselves underwater. Some have been observed to make three different kinds of sounds at the same time. They range in size from the giant Blue Whale, who makes sounds as low as twelve cycles per second, to small river dolphins in China and the Amazon, who can make sounds exceeding 200,000 cycles per second.

Some of the most complex sounds made by any living thing are the songs of the Humpback Whale. These animals sing their immensely loud sounds over vast distances of the sea. They appear to repeat the songs from year to year but with new variations. Groups of whales will collectively evolve these changes, taking up to eight years to completely alter a song through new incremental additions. Individual songs can be repeated for several hours at a time. Like ancient bards singing the tales of an aural tradition, or the languid phrases of a Bruckner symphony, they resonate the ocean floor to echo their deep and mysterious voices.

6 ALASKA: UNDERWATER WALRUS

Sometimes a researcher is lucky enough to happen onto sounds that are a total surprise. Les Gilbert recorded this group of walrus off the coast of Alaska. It is known that walrus have large sacs used for mysterious deep sea dives;

they may have something to do with how these sounds are made. This recording is an amazing curiousity. Even for someone who has had a lot of experience listening to animal sounds, the feeling of listening in on some sort of alien language is irresistible.

The philosopher Wittgenstein once said: "If a lion could talk, we could not understand him." He probably meant that the schism between human culture and the lion's world is so great that language cannot bridge the gap. It would be a language too foreign to us. What I like about this statement is how it respects the otherness of the animal world and recognizes how codes of communication, like these walrus sounds, arise from the unique organization of living things.

Science has begun to probe deeply into the possibility that our assumptions about animal intelligence and communication have been too simplistic. For centuries much of humanity has claimed superiority over the nonhuman world; our older models of evolution have guaranteed this view. The justification for this argument was often based upon an assumption that since animals did not possess language, they were simply organic machines to be ruthlessly exploited. New evidence suggests that thinking does not require language in human terms and that each form of life may have its own way of being self-aware. Life and cognition might be considered synonymous even at the cellular level.

We can embrace the alien for its right to exist without destroying it or demanding that it either serve us or exhibit human traits. Along with humans, other forms of life exist as co-conspirators in a mystery of which we only have a small glimpse. One important feature of their being alien is that they are part of a puzzle through which we can explore a sense of self that transcends the human.

7 SMOKEY MOUNTAINS, NORTH CAROLINA: FROGS

There are thousands of species of amphibians all over the world. They were probably the first animals with a spine to crawl out of watery environments to live on land, approx-imately 335 million years ago. While a couple types of salamanders have been heard to make faint noises, frogs and toads are the real sound-makers. Most have a mem-brane that functions like a primitive eardrum right at the side of their heads. Frogs produce sounds for a surprising range of purposes: distress calls, mating calls, territorial defense, and calls to trigger gathering. Every species of frog has a distinct call or calls. There can also be variations in calls, similar to human accents, among the same species based upon geographic separation.

In this recording we can hear a distinct assortment of frogs that demonstrates the different pitch distributions of various species. Try to count how many different kinds there are and how their calls differ.

This recording is an example of how we can sometimes bear witness to small dramas in nature. The recording tells a story that we can easily follow. It's one of those unpredictable events that some people call a "Zen moment" when you just happen to be at the right point in the time/space continuum or perhaps, more accurately, you are attuned to what's really going on around you. Here it's the relationship of predator to prey. Listen closely and you can track the bird's movement in the stereo field between your loudspeakers. If you close your eyes you can even imagine it in flight above you.

This is also a good demonstration of how sound articulates the relationship between things, particularly how sound is meaningful about the unfolding of time. If we only saw the raven fly over, without hearing its call or the sound of the invisible frogs, we would never know of their mutual awareness.

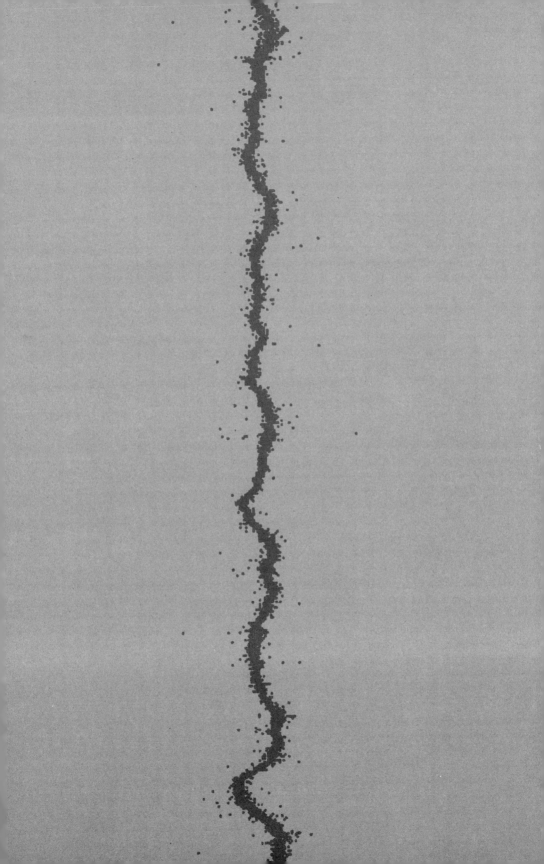

INSECTS AND FROGS

I recorded these sounds at night from a small boat deep in the Atchafalaya Swamp, the largest fresh water swamp in North America. While recording I would shine a flashlight on the water surface to reveal multiple pairs of red alligator eyes looking up from below. This soundscape is just one of a variety that could have been recorded from the same location at different times over the course of one night. A particular chorus will continue for hours and then gradually go silent at a future point in time. After a brief period of relative calm, another group of sound-makers will start up with a very different aggregate of sounds.

It's hard to listen to the immense complexity of this recording, with all of its variety and sheer number of frogs, and realize that frogs all over the planet are suddenly disappearing. Whole species have vanished without explanation in recent years. Biologists have guessed that this is due to a variety of environmental factors such as acid rain, increased pollutants, depletion of the atmosphere's ozone layer, or a combination of these factors. What we do know is that amphibians are particularly vulnerable to changes in their environment, and that the variety of species diminishing over a wide geographic area suggests that whatever is happening is global in scale.

IRANGI, ZAIRE: INSECTS AND FROGS

Here is another dense fabric of night sounds made up of insects and frogs. Listen to the overall density of sound and its subtle shifting patterns. If you pay close attention you can distinguish that what at first appears to be a single thick tapestry of sound is made up of discernible layers, each from a distinct creature or group of such creatures. While they might all seem to interlock into one large texture, they also form subsidiary lines and sub-patterns that appear and disappear.

43

Examples eleven and twelve are directly related by the fact that they are two different recordings of the same exact location, a watering hole in an African game park. The microphones weren't moved an inch. These illustrate how distinct the soundscape can be at different times of day and night. You've surely noticed similarly distinct soundscapes at different times of day where you live. Perhaps these examples will inspire you to pay closer attention to the details of your own shifting sound world.

44

The first recording was made in the early evening after most of the large game animals had dispersed. The frogs and insects created a consistent audible tapestry throughout the night that was occasionally contributed to by larger mammals like hippos or this lion. Apparently he was a solitary male who had lost dominance over his pride to another male. His mournful roar went on for hours.

12 MASUMA PAN, HWANGE, ZIMBABWE:

MORNING SOUNDS

The next morning produced this soundscape that shares nothing with the sounds of the previous night except the lonely lion. A new congregation of high-pitched insects has taken over and the morning birds have replaced the amphibians. There are a few unusual sounds here that require close attention. The low frequency drone that is reminiscent of a motor humming was produced by hundreds of low-flying scarab beetles above the water surface.

If you listen even closer you can hear something like water running. This is the sound of a kerosene-driven pump that brings water up from the aquifer below. These pumps are a common feature in many game parks that have resulted from the artificial boundaries imposed upon the wildlife by man. Without them much of the wildlife would perish. At first I found their presence to be a real disturbance to my wild safari fantasy. Later I understood that Africa is no different from the rest of the Earth's fast transition of wilderness into global park. The important thing to understand is not only how humanity has radically altered the biosphere but the depth of the responsibility we now carry for its future survival.

13 **BOSQUE DEL APACHE, NEW MEXICO:**

INSECTS AND BIRDS

Bio-acousticians have theorized that many locations on Earth, where living things reside, have a unique biospectrum, a recognizable pattern to the sounds of that place. Furthermore these patterns may be stable over time, shifting with the time of day or from season to season, but if you return at a specific hour on a specific day, you hear something almost identical with the way it was the year before. This may have important implications for how we diagnose changes in the ecological health of biohabitats. It is particularly interesting when you consider how short the life-span can be for individual members of certain species. The biospectrum remains stable though it consists of new members constantly replacing old ones. The chorus of sound might also generate information about the whole ecosystem that is recognized and responded to by the individual members of the co-existing whole.

What might the dense audible biospectrum of this record-ing tell us? In many ways the density seems unnatural if you know anything about the broader terrain that sur-rounds this wildlife preserve. It is the New Mexico desert where things are usually pretty quiet. This preserve, how-ever, is an artificial construct placed there as part of a net-work of similar habitat islands for migrating birds. In some ways it is a concentration camp demanded by dwindling habitat. There are a few endangered species that have been heard here, including the rare Whooping Crane.

14 THE COTSWALDS, ENGLAND: BIRDS

In contrast to the many wilderness recording sites includ-ed in this book, this recording was made in a location that many people consider a quintessential example of the English countryside. With its rolling meadows and beech forests, the Cotswalds is a splendid sample of what remains of the natural environment in Western Europe. Wildlife and song birds have adapted long ago to this intensely "humanized" environment. Despite there being over four thousand years of visible history in this land-scape, there is also a deep concern for what remains of the non-human. The Cotswalds is an extraordinary example of how human habitation can be harmoniously merged into the natural world.

ISLAND OF ELBA, ITALY: DAWN CHORUS

This dawn chorus on the Tuscan archipelago of Elba was recorded from the top of a hillside near the town of Marciana Marina. Through the dense early morning mist you can hear a typical assortment of European and Mediterranean birds greeting the day. Besides its beautiful beach towns, across the island there are many small villages nestled into a continuous blanket of forest. The casual visitor might never suspect that most of these trees are fairly new arrivals, the island having been originally deforested to fuel ancient iron ore smelters thousands of years ago. I can only imagine that these birds are grateful for the return of lush vegetation to this island.

KAKADU, AUSTRALIA: BIRDS

One property of insect sounds and bird calls that we are just beginning to understand is their great variety. Why are there so many diverse forms of communication among these creatures, and why do they vary so from place to place? In many environments visual communication takes on a subsidiary role, at least at distances beyond the close intimacy of mates or members within a group. The diversity of auditory signals must arise so as to differentiate themselves within a dense fabric of sound. The morphology of a specific call may evolve as a kind of terracing effect such that each finds a particular level or niche to fit within.

49

Now listen to this recording from the NorthernTerritory of Australia. Notice the wide variety of calls but also how their novelty unfolds within a particular temporal cycle. It's as if there is only a certain density allowed before someone makes room for something else. The sound is continuous and dense but every signal can be distinctly apprehended. It is suggestive of just how aware the total mesh of sound-makers must be of each other.

LAUNCHING PLACE, AUSTRALIA:

LYREBIRDS AND RAINFALL

Here is an example of a temperate forest in southeastern Australia. Notice how the quality of sound is thick from the cold temperature and moisture in the air. In this environment too, the density of vegetation requires the primacy of auditory signals for communication over distance, but with different results. The population of larger animals is not very dense, so there is much less variety of signals. One of the principal denizens of this environment is the

Lyrebird, so named because of the shape of its tail feathers. Seldom seen, and even less often recorded, they are the objects of many apocryphal stories about their spectacular ability of sound mimicry: surprised lumberjacks fleeing from birds making chainsaw sounds and that sort of thing.

These were recorded at dawn at the home of my friend, the composer/poet Chris Mann. In the great tradition of Australian story telling, Chris has perfected many Lyrebird yarns, encouraging some to take on the patina of folk myths. My favorite is about his Polish neighbor, who for years would swear at the noisy Lyrebirds until one day the forest responded back to him with a chorus of Slavic swear words.

Whether the stories are true or not, Lyrebirds are brilliant mimics, so much so that I've wondered if their name was some naturalist's spelling error. What this also alludes to is the illusory side of sound. Sometimes things do not sound as they should, but real instances of aural camouflage by animals are very rare. Humans are the masters of this and have probably used the imitation of wildlife sounds to lure prey since they began hunting many thousands of years ago. Now we have tape recorders that only compound the illusions. Listen to the rain in this recording and how it sounds like fire.

TIERRA DEL FUEGO, CHILE:

MAGELLANIC PENGUINS AND CORMORANTS

Listen to the visceral power in the calls of these large sea birds and how the sounds express the mutual awareness of the gathered birds.

The hearing of birds is similar to our own – they were probably the first animals to evolve a cochlea in the inner ear. They mostly have excellent hearing, but this varies a lot through a range of unique specializations. Birds of prey such as eagles and owls may have the most sensitive hearing. All birds vocalize through a soundbox called a syrinx at the bottom of their windpipe. Actually, not all birds make sounds; some vultures, for instance, make none at all. Most birds do, and the more complex their vocal apparatus, the more ornate is their song. The syrinx is basically a cartilage structure containing membranes that vibrate with air. The bird contracts and expands adjacent muscles to form the sound of its voice. Birds produce these sounds for purposes that include both individual needs and behaviors relevant for the survival of the species. Songs and calls have been observed in relation to mating, warning, distress, identification, territorial claims, courtship, aggression, social bonding, nest building, flocking, and cries of hunger by the young. Even the lowly chicken is known to possess a large vocabulary of sounds.

19   RED ROCK LAKES, MONTANA: BIRDS AND INSECTS

Generally speaking, the difference between a bird call and a song is fairly simple. Songs have distinct pitches or tones that conform to a definite pattern. They can be very ornate vocalizations or simpler repetitions of a few tones, but usually feel purposefully arranged. Calls, on the other hand, are mostly simple and brief without complex repetition or patterning. This distinction is not always clear-cut, since calls and songs can often occur in rapid succession. One thing that is now well understood is that bird songs are a combination of acquired learning and inborn components. Birds learn parts of their song from their mature associates but use only those sounds for which they have been innately programmed.

In this example we can hear a variety of different birds flying across the surface of a small lake, towards or away from the surrounding shore.

ANZA-BORREGO DESERT, CALIFORNIA:
INSECTS AND BIRDS

At the opposite extreme from rainforests are the Earth's ever enlarging desert habitats. In these environments, the lack of moisture demands that vegetation be sparse and that its large animals become rugged and widely dispersed. In such a habitat there is not extreme competition to find an available slot in the sonic fabric. Sounds also don't need to be loud, since they can carry over a large distance without interference. I once performed a large sound composition very near to where this recording was made and was later told by visitors that they heard it from over two miles away.

Listen to the quiescent quality of this sample and the resonance surrounding the songs of distant birds.

Despite the special beauty that desert habitats exhibit, there is a real danger in the trend of many continents toward increasing desertification. While the situation in North Africa is well known, with its devastating droughts and disappearance of wildlife habitat, it is not so widely known that some ecologists believe that areas of desertification in the American southwest are expanding faster than in North Africa.

21

DISTIN LAKE, ALASKA: LOONS

Their are several ways that bird-watchers identify species. Visual cues such as coloration, size, flight pattern and the shape of wings are important, but so are the songs and calls they make. When you realize that there are almost 9,000 different kinds of birds in the world, each ornithologist can only recognize a limited number of species and their individual variations through sound. Some, however, are so distinct that there is no ambiguity about them. The loon is a good example. Listen to its yodeling call that is both mournful and reminiscent of laughter. Also listen to the beautiful echo in this example, that articulates a sense of large open space.

56

CHAMA, NEW MEXICO: HUMMINGBIRD

Sometimes other sounds besides vocalization can be used to distinguish between similar species of birds. Hummingbirds are so-named because of the humming sound produced by their wings. The male Broad-tailed hummingbird can be recognized by the metallic whistle of its wings. Otherwise it is almost indistinguishable from the Ruby-throated hummingbird, its common neighbor to the east of the Rockies. The female is virtually impossible to differentiate from several other species. This little fellow exhibited the typical hummingbird trait of fearlessly pursuing a food source even as I shoved microphones at it that were ten times its size.

23 **YAKUSHIMA FOREST, JAPAN: INSECTS AND BIRDS**

This exquisite recording of a Japanese forest soundscape is not only provocative for the beauty of the nature sounds but also for how it is suggestive of aspects of Japanese culture. I hear things in this recording that are so much a part of how I think about traditional Japan. The sense of time, its slow pulse and purposefulness, is directly evocative of Japanese music such as Gagaku. In fact, Japanese musicians claim that the relationship is the other way around: the music evolved from meditative listening to nature. Listen to the juxtaposition of the extended bird songs against the abrupt singularity of others, or the simple but elegant pitch inflections against the accelerating rhythm of a single pulsing call.

RAINFOREST, INDONESIA:

NIGHT SOUNDS AND THUNDERSTORM

The largest numbers of different kinds of species occur in the tropical rainforest habitats of the Earth, where the vegetation is incredibly dense. These areas contain two-thirds of the world's flowering plants, and the number of different species of trees in a few acres can surpass that of the entire continent of Europe. One hectare of the Borneo forest can contain 400 types of trees. Just as the flora is rich in species, so is the fauna. A six square mile area on Barro Colorado in the Panama Canal Zone supports 20,000 species of insects, compared to only a few hundred in the entirety of France.

As one might suspect, the denizens of the rainforest create the most densely layered natural soundscape. The anthropologist and musician Steven Feld describes the New Guinea rainforest as: "a world of coordinated sound clocks, an intersection of millions of simultaneous cycles all refusing to ever start or stop at the same point."

While the immense Amazonian rainforest is well known, this recording is of a less celebrated tropical rainforest, that of Malaysia and Indonesia. Although it is smaller than the Amazon Basin, it supports a huge diversity of unique forms of life and its sounds are just as rich and varied as other rainforests. It is also just as endangered. These sounds are quickly disappearing as commercial exploitation literally turns this rainforest into chopsticks.

25

SANGRE DE CRISTO MOUNTAINS, NEW MEXICO:

GREY SQUIRREL

One outstanding fact about the study of communication by land mammals is how little we really know about it, as compared to birds or many other smaller creatures. This is easy to explain – they are just harder to study. Most of the big predators are nocturnal or shy. Many are nomadic or difficult to approach. They also don't exhibit their full range of communicative behavior in captivity. In the wild, most land mammals possess very sensitive hearing and the sounds they produce have a wide assortment of char-acteristics. The sounds they make to threaten or intimidate are often very different from the sounds they make to attract a mate. Most of the land mammals, however, make sounds that can communicate over a distance. Some that are more social, or that congregate in herds, make sounds that help to organize group behavior. Two types of mammals use sound to orient their movement underwater or in darkness.

One way that land animals employ auditory signals is for

the proclamation of territorial boundaries. This example presents such an occasion, although I'm not sure if I was the cause of the disturbance or if another squirrel was threatening the vocalizer's food cache. The sound went on at this intensity for over thirty minutes and was in progress as I arrived on the scene.

Appreciation for the intelligence of squirrels has increased in recent years as more people have had the opportunity to observe and interact with these small mammals at the edges of suburban sprawl or in urban parks. Their exploits at backyard birdfeeders have become legendary, spawning a minor cottage industry in new birdfeeder designs that can thwart their ingenious ability to adapt to new circumstances. Researchers have observed the capacity of wild squirrels to persevere for weeks at a time, circumventing new obstacles put in the way of a desired food source. They will memorize complex adaptive strategies that are quickly shared with their comrades, employing their phenomenal gymnastic abilities to crawl on vertical surfaces, tightrope walk, leap with great agility, and in some cases glide through the air for huge distances.

26

MOSS LANDING, CALIFORNIA:

DAWN CHORUS AND RED FOX

The acuity of hearing possessed by many mammals is astonishing, at least when compared to our own. During the taping of this example I had remained stationary for over thirty minutes while recording the dawn chorus of birds. I was unaware of how close I was to the den of a fox until it started barking this alarm call. At first I thought it was scolding me. Then I realized that its big ears were responding to the intrusion of an approaching helicopter that neither I, nor my condenser microphones, had yet detected. Besides the admiration that this sensitive hearing can inspire in us, we also need to understand how this sensitivity makes many animals especially vulnerable to the sound pollution of human machines.

63

A frustrating aspect of wildlife sound recording is the inescapable presence of motor noise in our sound environment. The sounds of distant traffic, overhead aircraft and the roar of motor boats infect almost every biohabitat that I've visited. The effects of this ever increasing noise level upon many forms of life is growing more devastating every year. Many animals are simply driven from their habitat, which is already shrinking. That is, our sounds are factors in their own right in the destruction of habitat. Even more tragic is the effect on an animal like the manatee. Some researchers believe that many of these animals have become deaf from the unceasing cacophony of recreational motor boats. Since the animals can no longer hear their motors, they are killed by the fast moving vehicles. Likewise, the communication of whales, who previously could hear each other over hundreds of miles, is now frustrated by the underwater roar of human ocean traffic.

27 **RAINFOREST, COSTA RICA:**

HOWLER MONKEYS AND INSECTS

The study of primates has been motivated as much by a desire to learn about ourselves as by interest in their unique behaviors. Anthropologists have looked to the other primates for clues about the evolution of human societies. As our closest biological relatives, however, they are surprisingly less noisy than humans and do much of their communicating through visual gestures. This is especially true of the largest primates such as chimpanzees and gorillas who are less vulnerable to predators. Research into communication between humans and apes has revealed startling evidence about their ability to acquire basic language skills through visual signals. This predominance of visual over aural communication among other primates would appear to make our extensive use of sound through linguistic speech a unique adaptation. A rudimentary form of music, however, seems to exist among chimpanzees. Various researchers, including Jane van Lawick-Goodall and Vernon and Frances Reynolds, have observed drumming and "singing" festivals that can last for several hours.

The old and new world monkeys vocalize more than the larger apes. Some of the most audacious are the howler monkeys of Central and South America. Like all primates, including humans, they have a larynx and vocal membrane. Vocalization occurs when a column of air is forced through these organs by the respiratory muscles. Male howlers emit a chain of grunts in rapid succession when they want other members in their group to pay attention to them. When howler groups become excited they can continue vocalizing for up to four hours.

SONORAN DESERT, MEXICO:

MEXICAN WOLVES AND COYOTES

My colleague Jack Loeffler recorded this unusual example of interspecies communication while on one of his hiking trips in the Sonoran Desert of Mexico. Mexican wolves were on one side of a canyon and a pack of coyotes on the other. You can differentiate their calls if you listen carefully. The wolves have an elongated howl that starts high and drops in pitch. The coyotes are more boisterous with a yipping sound. Despite the geological and biological chasms that separate these two species, they seem to be having a very good time.

Since Jack made this recording, the Mexican wolf is no longer found here. This is an example of a sound no longer audible in the wild. Attempts to reintroduce wolves bred in captivity have started in wilderness areas of the southwestern United States but what success they will have remains to be heard.

CARLSBAD CAVERNS, NEW MEXICO:

INTERIOR SOUNDS

Now we are inside the Earth, miles deep in an immense underground cavern. We are in total darkness. The sounds here are rarely of living things. Only drips of water are audible, and sometimes the creaking of the cave walls. Some things do live here and some even make sound, but mostly for a different purpose than other mammals do. This is the home of the second most numerous mammal on our planet, the bat.

Bats are truly magical creatures that have been needlessly

persecuted. Rather than dangerous vermin, they are mostly shy and docile animals of tremendous benefit to nature and humanity. For example, the colony of twenty million Mexican freetail bats that live in Bracken Cave, Texas, consume over a quarter of a million pounds of insects each night. Bats account for one-fourth of all mammal species, with nearly 1,000 different kinds. Contrary to absurd popular myths, in the United States only .5 % of bats carry the rabies virus, much less than cats or dogs. Only fifteen people in the last forty years died from any bat-related disease, and these were mostly due to their handling obviously sick animals. Fifteen people die every year from dog attacks, but nobody would propose to wipe out dogs in the same way that bats have been needlessly destroyed.

NOTE:

You can listen to a continuous sequence of the cave and bat sounds by selecting track 29. Allow the disc to play through to the end of example 32. You also can listen to each example separately, stopping it when the index number changes.

CARLSBAD CAVERNS, NEW MEXICO:

ENTRANCE TO BAT ROOKERY

In Carlsbad Caverns National Park there lives a large colony of Mexican freetail bats. The colony consists of approximately one million individuals that roost together on the ceiling and walls of a large cavern chamber. Perhaps the most amazing characteristic of most bats is the sounds they make. Like cetaceans and some night flying birds, bats can "see" with their ears through a process similar to sonar, called echolocation. This adaptation allows these animals to move about in total darkness and hunt insects with precise accuracy. Echolocation works through the bat emitting very high frequency chirping sounds, way above the hearing range of human ears, that are reflected back from an object or surface to the bat's ears. The animal compares these reflected sounds with the sounds it continues to emit and processes what the differences tell it about its surroundings. Many researchers now believe that this aural orientation skill is so precise that its results may be mentally equivalent to a visual image.

In this recording we can hear the wing motion of the bats as they fly through darkness above my head. We can barely discern the sounds of their high frequency chirps. These sounds are mostly out of the range of our hearing but once in awhile the pitch descends just into the upper limit of what we can distinguish from the rushing sounds of flight. At this point in their nightly exit from the caverns they have just left the rookery and are moving toward the main entrance.

31 **CARLSBAD CAVERNS, NEW MEXICO:**

BATS LEAVING MAIN ENTRANCE

During the winter the bats live in Mexico; they return to Carlsbad in the late spring. The bats fly out of the cavern entrance in a huge spiraling column, one continuous cloud of flying mammals. This allows them to gain suffi-cient lift to fly out into the dusk sky, flying over fifty miles each night in search of insects. We can hear the sound of this mass flight as an immense disruption of air, through which the bats gain speed with each turn of the ascending spiral.

CARLSBAD CAVERNS, NEW MEXICO: BATS RETURNING

The bats remain outside all night to feed and begin to return to the cave just before sunrise. They return individually, flying straight into the cave entrance at over sixty miles per hour. The whirring sounds in this example are made by the single bats as they come in high and dive in quickly with half-folded wings. You can just make out the distant sound of their echolocation chirps as they hit the cave's interior darkness.

33

MORA, NEW MEXICO: UNDERWATER POND INSECTS

Obviously there are a huge variety of insect sounds, but

the ways that they produce these is also surprisingly diverse. They include: tapping, wing vibration, wing buzzing, wing clicking, drumming, stridulation, rasping, expulsion of air or liquid, snapping, and buzzing. Sometimes these sounds can even be useful to humans. Everyone is familiar with the chirrups of crickets, but one species, the Snowy Tree Cricket, can be used to calculate the temperature outdoors. You count the number of chirrups in fifteen seconds and add forty to get the degrees in Fahrenheit.

I've inserted this collage of underwater insect sounds between the sounds of mammals and humans for a reason: to remind us that intelligence can reside in unlikely places. We usually associate the intelligence of life forms with how big they are, or with their proximity to us on the evolutionary tree. The tiny size and alien quality of insects and spiders presents us with a challenge. How could they possess anything but the most rudimentary of mental functions, tiny automatons without thought or feeling? The amazing sophistication of social insects betrays this assumption. Ant societies are particularly impressive, while the observed behavior of bee colonies has taken on mythic proportions. There are even a few types of social spiders who build such large communal webs that people in Mexico will bring them inside to serve as natural fly-paper during fly season. We know that bees communicate a large range of information about the details of their environment through dance (along with sound and smell). While this "waggle dance" is regarded as the only insect "language" yet known, there are clues that others await discovery. One candidate is a water beetle of the genus Berosus. These little critters appear to have a vocabulary of faint sounds that they emit underwater for purposes of warning and mating.

An important scientific concept of the later 20th century has been the idea of emergent properties: patterns can arise from a complex process that appear to transcend the agents that bring the process into being. When viewed from this perspective, individual bees probably can be understood as parts of a collective mind. The hive is an intelligent organism emergent from the total activities of its cellular bee members. Perhaps it's easier to grasp this idea if you consider that an average hive consists of close to 50,000 bees that collectively weigh about ten pounds. That collective brain is not only capable of communication with itself, but also disperses its cellular members over a large geographic space.

I first started making these underwater insect recordings by accident. On a recording expedition, while waiting to be picked up by my associates, I had nothing to record after the dawn chorus had ended. To alleviate the boredom I threw my hydrophones into a small pond and was astounded at the resultant noise level in the water. After a couple years of listening to these small ponds and marshes, I came to understand a pattern to their underwater sound-making. I even put together a small aquarium populated with the typical creatures I found in the wild. A few would make tentative sounds in captivity but many would not. At least I was able to verify that the sounds were mostly made by these tiny insects. The one consistent factor is how beautiful and complex these miniature sounds are. I have finally reconciled myself to the gut feeling that these sounds are an emergent property of the pond. Something that speaks as a collective voice for a mind that is beyond my grasp. I know that this is not a scientific way of thinking, but I can't help myself. Now when I see a pond, I think of the water's surface as a membrane enclosing something deep in thought.

34

BESA VILLAGE, ZIMBABWE: NIGHT SOUNDS

Now we hear a human habitation wedged between the African wilderness and a two lane paved highway that serves as a major trucking route. The length of this example is just about the average time between passing vehicles. In the foreground are various nocturnal insects. In the distance are frogs and the village ambience itself: voices, drums and a braying donkey. This recording reinforces one of the most powerful impressions I had of the relationship between African culture and environment: an overwhelming sense of the persistence of spirit as an intrinsic component of the African ecology. For many African people the sounds of animals are not merely the calls of separate organisms. They are the voice of a spirit form resident in that individual but also present in all the members of its species. That spirit is like a persistent and collective intelligence that defies geographic separation.

This concept of spirit is not only present in the beliefs of the traditional religious practices but appears as an essential trait of domestic life. It can even be understood to include the influence of the dead (both human and animal) as a resonance from the past that not only informs all aspects of daily life but is essential to the vitality and interaction of all living things.

Most of us live in cities or in circumstances where our daily sound environment consists almost entirely of human made sounds: traffic, people talking, office machines, television and radio. If we do live where the sounds of crickets and birds still occur, we are seldom aware of them and they merely take on the quality of something happening at the periphery of consciousness, subliminal at best.

What I like about this recording is how it places the

human world into a larger frame. The sounds of human speech and laughter, or the noises of domestic life, can be heard as something within a bigger pattern of life. They are part of the mix and not something that dominates the fabric. Many traditional cultures have maintained a balance that you can hear. You can physically stand between the human community on one side and the communities of nonhuman intelligence on the other.

CHIMAYÓ, NEW MEXICO:
FROGS, INSECTS AND TRAFFIC

This recording of a summer night in a small traditional Northern New Mexico village also happens to be the sounds of my own backyard. Chimayó's European settlement dates back to the 18th century, and the structure where I live is part of the old plaza and fortress of its original Spanish inhabitants. Nearby is the famous *Santuario de Chimayó* where the legend of its holy dirt attracts people from all over the world to seek healing. On this particular night you can hear the resident frogs in my neighbor's pond and a variety of local dogs. You can also hear night insects in the nearby chile fields. Eventually the calm is disturbed by another neighbor's ornately painted "low rider" car, wending its way through the village.

36 **VONDELPARK, AMSTERDAM, NETHERLANDS:**

PARK SOUNDS

These sounds are fairly typical of a weekday morning in one of the major public parks of Europe. As one of the great utopian "green" spaces, Vondelpark is home to a rich assortment of birds and other wildlife that survive within the center of the large urban area of Amsterdam. The park is obviously also a nexus for recreational and commuting activity by human residents and tourists. On this particular morning you can hear birds and a variety of people strolling and riding bicycles along the many park pathways.

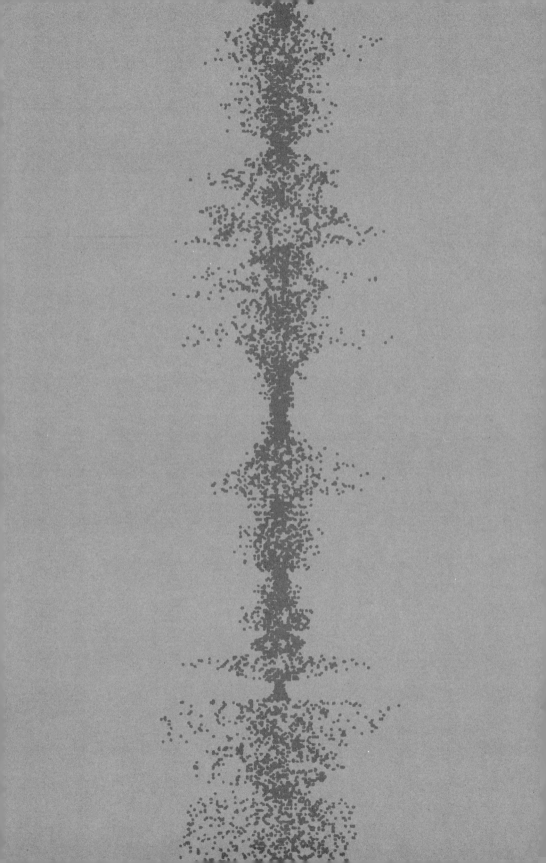

I made this curious recording as part of a commercial assignment for a science museum. I needed the real world sounds of a variety of bicycle wheels in motion in order to illustrate through sound the relative qualities of new bicycle wheel design features. Luckily, a major race was scheduled close to home and I was able to set up my microphones to catch the dynamic effect of passing cyclists. I find this recording interesting for its particular psychological attributes. To me the sounds of the bicycles seem delicate and almost fragile, especially when compared to other human mechanical technologies. How amazing that only a century ago this technology personified speed and the transcendence of human physiology through the machine, whereas now it represents a rare opportunity to admire human strength freed from reliance on machines.

38

SANTA MONICA PIER: ARCADE AND STREET SOUNDS

In contrast to the sonic tapestries of the non-human world, this free-for-all of video games, pinball machines, and street commotion sounds as if hardly any component is listening to another. What emerges from this uniquely human aggregate of noise-making are sonic patterns of disintegrated mind that seem peculiar to our species. What an odd contradiction that so much intelligence, in the form of people and technology, is harnessed to produce a soundscape that is so without apparent integration. However, despite the negative sentiments that I'm expressing, I must admit that I made this recording because of the pure exhiliration that these sounds evoke.

39

KALANGA VILLAGE, ZIMBABWE: GLOSSOLALIA

It might be argued that there are many sounds made by humans that are somewhere between speech and singing. 20th century artists, in particular, have explored the purposeful confusion between these modes of vocalization from both literary and musical approaches. A more ancient form of vocal communication that is in between speech and song is glossolalia or speaking-in-tongues. It is one of the most universal of trance induction techniques. Glossolalia is found all over the world and exhibits similar characteristics no matter the culture or language spoken.

Listen to this example of glossolalia from the edge of an African desert. It isn't singing but it isn't really speech either. It makes me wonder what it is about these phenomena that allows us to place them into different categories in the first place.

One way of thinking about the apparently distinct categories our brains use for organizing different kinds of sounds, is a model proposed by composer Warren Burt. While this is hardly a scientific hypothesis, I find it useful as a working model until we learn more about psychoacoustics in this area. It resonates with my personal experience and may be all I have to go on for now.

The idea is that sounds somehow get classified into three major areas of experience. Apparently we need to place what we hear into one of these categories so as to assign it meaning. We call the languages we understand speech, the noises of nature or the city, environmental sound, and the sounds that usually form harmonic/melodic patterns, music.

Some aspect of these distinctions might be hard-wired into our brains just like the way birds only learn sounds that trigger innate properties. Whatever is innate to the structure of our brains, however, we also seem capable of a wide range of flexibility, since most of us shift sounds from one category to another over the course of our lives. When we first hear the sounds of a foreign language we usually process it as unintelligible noise. We can recognize that it is being spoken by another person but the sounds have no meaning, or a limited range of meaning like the sounds of the environment. If we learn to speak that language, the sounds get reclassified into the intelligible speech category as distinct from environmental sounds or music.

Much of the experimental work with sound done by

artists in this century has been about exploring the reclassification of different sounds from one category into another and of the transitional zones between them. For many people there is some anxiety associated with hearing a piece of music that falls outside their previous experience of musicality, especially experimental music or music from another culture. For them it is not music and they will often call it noise. This doesn't mean that it cannot be reclassified with greater exposure or understanding. The history of western music might support this. Many innovations in music composition that were originally rejected by critics and audiences are now regarded as masterpieces.

What my own experience has taught me is that listenings associated with these different modes of sound classification carry with them different states of consciousness. Our ability to shift these modes, and float between them, makes available a vast domain of states of awareness and potential realities.

My hunch is that something like this complex mirroring process through sound was the origin of human music. Indeed, perhaps music has been our species' way of retaining a mode of consciousness that is similar to how mind is organized in the nonhuman world.

The fact that every culture has some form of music speaks to its universal significance for human beings, although I think that this is mostly an unconscious significance. For the most part we really don't know what music is. Lewis Thomas tells the story of the German government plan to fund the next Max Planck Institute and of the committee that was organized to formulate the important research question that could justify the institute as its central purpose. After much debate the committee proposed that the institute address the mystery of what music is and why humans need it. Unfortunately, the German government declined.

Since no scientific institute has attempted to grapple with this question, I feel justified in my wild speculations. I think music may be a conservation strategy for keeping something alive that we may now need to make more conscious. A way of making sense of the world from which we might refashion our relationship to nonhuman living systems. I wonder if music might be our way of mapping reality through metaphors of sound, as if it were a way of thinking that is parallel to the visually dominant metaphors of our speech and written symbols.

I think that most musicians can relate to this idea. Music is not just something that we do to amuse ourselves – it is a different way of thinking about the world. A way of thinking that we probably share with dolphins and wolves. It also might be a way to remind ourselves of a prior wholeness when the spirit of the forest was not something out there, separate in the world, but something of which we were an intrinsic part.

This recording is of children singing. Like children everywhere they sing without self-consciousness as an expression of delight in themselves and the group to which they also give voice. Their joy is both individual and collective, a

87

joy that emanates from the soil that they cultivate, the air they breathe, and the voices of other life that surrounds them.

SUMMARY

After listening to all these sounds and what I have to say about them, you might still be wondering why I think it's so important to convince you of the need to be more conscious of how we hear things. While I do believe that shifting away from visual dominance toward an increased aural focus on the world around us changes our behavior in positive ways, I'll let other people grind that particular axe. I'd rather discuss a few other things that might affirm the need for what I'm talking about.

I've already discussed the quality of integrative perception that sound engenders so allow me to summarize that argument. Put simply, what we hear from other forms of life, and the environment they reside in, is information that

88

is unique and essential about patterns of relationship in context. It is an experiential basis from which we can shape an understanding of the "integrated fabric of mind that envelops us."

For example, an important innovation of 20th century music has been the "emancipation of noise" so often associated with the composer John Cage. He and many other musicians have sought to expand the resources of music beyond the vocabulary of pitch and harmony that had previously defined it. Through the "musical" manipulation of the noises of everyday life they achieved an understanding of the meaning of these sounds as aesthetic phenomena, opportunities for a deepened awareness of the world we live in. Perhaps because of this contribution to art we now can understand the need to extend it further. The sounds of living things are not just a resource for manipulation – they are evidence of mind in nature and patterns of communication with which we share a common bond and meaning.

Attentive listening to the sounds around us is one of the

most venerable forms of meditative practice. This receptive yet focused listening can concentrate awareness on where and what we are and quiet the incessant internal chatter of the mind. The experience is grounded in a dance between separation and interconnection, revelation and mystery, pattern and novelty. Through enlivening our ears and engaging in more attentive listening, we are drawn deeper into a resonance with life itself, a place of wonder where we might begin to ask questions like, why do whales and children sing?

RECORDING CREDITS

David Dunn

Tracks 1, 2, 3, 7, 8, 9, 11, 12, 13, 15, 17, 19, 20, 22, 25, 26, 29, 30, 31, 32, 33, 34, 35, 36, 37, 38, 39, 40

Les Gilbert

Tracks 4, 5, 6, 10, 14, 16, 18, 21, 23, 24, 27

Jack Loeffler

Track 28*

DAVID DUNN is an internationally recognized composer, performer, theorist and sound designer. His compositions and recordings have appeared in hundreds of concerts, exhibitions, video and film soundtracks, radio broadcasts, and in bioacoustic research. The author/editor of several books and numerous professional publications on music and the arts, his recordings include: *Angels and Insects* (O.O. Discs), *The Lion in Which the Spirits of the Royal Ancestors Make Their Home* (IML); and *Music, Language and Environment* (Innova). Currently he resides in New Mexico where he teaches at the College of Santa Fe and lives with his wife, daughter, two dachshunds and five birds.

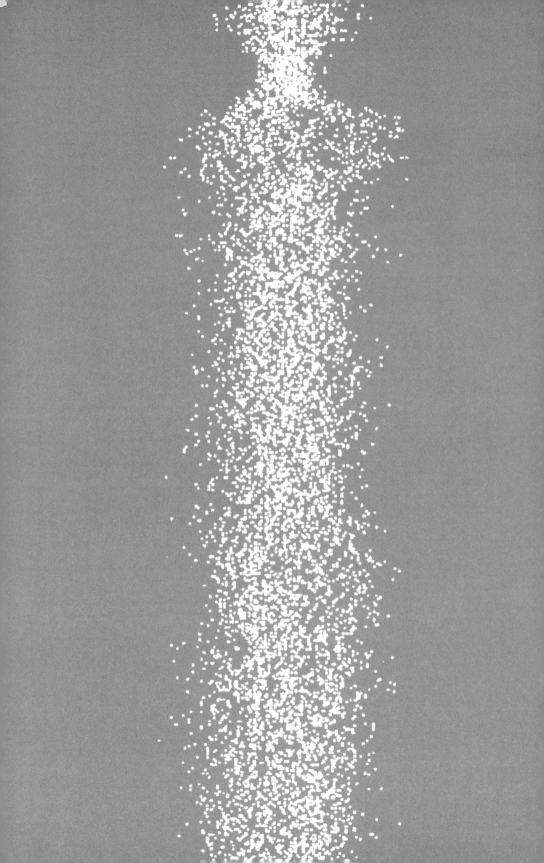

The Eternal Story, in its Original Language

EarthEar gathers together, for the first time, the work of the world's premier nature sound recordists and soundscape producers. Our goal is to help bring soundscape art into public awareness as a creative medium, in much the way photography emerged in the 1920's. EarthEar is releasing new CDs, offering a catalog of the best works available, and putting together a web site rich in context and connection with others in the field.

NEW CD RELEASES

93

THE DREAMS OF GAIA *(2 CDs, 48 page booklet)*
Featuring the work of 16 soundscape producers
This specially priced set offers a rich introduction to the field of soundscape recording and composition. Disc 1 is a real ear-opener, featuring surprising and engaging natural soundscapes, two excursions into urban soundings, and a taste of composing with transformed field recordings. Disc 2 is more subtle, asking the listener to enter into a state of "deep listening". It features longer cuts, arranged as a day cycle, from pre-dawn to the middle of the night, with each voicing of the planet being long enough to begin to cast its own particular spell. Here, you'll get a better sense of the deeper purposes behind the work of this group of extraordinary listener/composers.

FORESTS: A BOOK OF HOURS

Produced and composed by Douglas Quin

Forests is a groundbreaking combination of field recordings from forests in Madagascar, Africa, and South America, interwoven with sections of composed and improvised music that evoke deeper connections and attune our ears to the languages of nature. Even much of the "nature" material is composed of disparate but related recordings. Among the highlights are several African choral pieces, a trans-Atlantic meeting of primates, and the nearly seamless transitions between the musics of nature and man.

A DAY OF SOUND

Produced by Jason Reinier

On February 17, 1996 Jason encouraged recordists around the world to tape their surroundings. Over 40 did, and from the results, he's woven a 24-hour sound portrait of our planet. An 8-minute version aired on All Things Considered just over a year later. The sounds of both nature and humanity are included, often blurring the imaginary distinction between the two. The day is presented as one continuous piece, with passages that range from 30 seconds to 3 minutes. It is, literally, the most everyday nature sound disc ever, quite familiar and ordinary, yet its global reach offers a striking synergy.

THE CALL OF HOME is the first catalog to present a richly annotated introduction to the best back titles of more than 25 sound artists. It also includes an overview of styles, and artist bios. Our Core Library of 10 titles, available individually or by subscription, presents the cream of the crop, with examples of most of the stylistic approaches and a good variety of locales. Call 888-564-3399 for a copy of either the full Call of Home or Core Library catalog.

EarthEar.com

Visit EarthEar.com for an on-line version of The Call of Home catalog, sound samples, and ordering information. You'll also find our site to be a wide-ranging introduction to the themes and personalities that form the foundation of this emerging field, including essays, artist profiles, soundscape news, and links to groups working to further soundscape art and raise public awareness of soundscape issues in both urban and wilderness contexts.

95

E A R T H E A R

Enter a world where listening is an art…
and the voice of the planet is the muse.

YOUR EARS WILL NEVER BE THE SAME.

45 Cougar Canyon   Santa Fe, New Mexico 87505
888.564.3399

TRACK LIST

1 Chama, New Mexico: *Birds and Thunderstorm*
2 Venice, California: *Thunderstorm*
3 Les Moulins, Swiss Alps: *Cows and Thunderstorm*
4 Great Barrier Reef: *Underwater Sounds*
5 Maui, Hawaii: *Humpback Whales*
6 Round Island, Alaska: *Underwater Walrus*
7 Smokey Mountains, North Carolina: *Frogs*
8 Black Lakes, New Mexico: *Frogs and Ravens*
9 Atchafalaya Swamp, Louisiana: *Insects and Frogs*
10 Irangi, Zaire: *Insects and Frogs*
11 Masuma Pan, Hwange, Zimbabwe: *Night Sounds*
12 Masuma Pan, Hwange, Zimbabwe: *Morning Sounds*
13 Bosque del Apache, New Mexico: *Insects and Birds*
14 The Cotswalds, England: *Birds*
15 Island of Elba, Italy: *Dawn Chorus*
16 Kakadu, Australia: *Birds*
17 Launching Place, Australia: *Lyrebirds and Rainfall*
18 Tierra del Fuego, Chile: *Magellanic Penguins and Cormorants*
19 Red Rock Lakes, Montana: *Birds and Insects*
20 Anza-Borrego Desert, California: *Insects and Birds*
21 Distin Lake, Alaska: *Loons*
22 Chama, New Mexico: *Hummingbird*
23 Yakushima Forest, Japan: *Insects and Birds*
24 Rainforest, Indonesia: *Night Sounds and Thunderstorm*
25 Sangre de Cristo Mountains, New Mexico: *Grey Squirrel*
26 Moss Landing, California: *Dawn Chorus and Red Fox*
27 Rainforest, Costa Rica: *Howler Monkeys and Insects*
28 Sonoran Desert, Mexico: *Mexican Wolves and Coyotes*
29 Carlsbad Caverns, New Mexico: *Interior Sounds*
30 Carlsbad Caverns, New Mexico: *Entrance to Bat Rookery*
31 Carlsbad Caverns, New Mexico: *Bats Leaving Main Entrance*
32 Carlsbad Caverns, New Mexico: *Bats Returning*
33 Mora, New Mexico: *Underwater Pond Insects*
34 Besa Village, Zimbabwe: *Night Sounds*
35 Chimayo, New Mexico: *Frogs, Insects, and Traffic*
36 Vondelpark, Amsterdam, Netherlands: *Street Sounds*
37 Lake Cochiti, New Mexico: *Bicycle Race*
38 Santa Monica Pier, California: *Arcade and Street Sounds*
39 Kalanga Village, Zimbabwe: *Glossolalia*
40 Besa Village, Zimbabwe: *Children Singing*